MW00422933

The Nonconformist's Memorial

BOOKS BY SUSAN HOWE

Hinge Picture, Telephone Books, 1974
The Western Borders, Tuumba Press, 1979
Secret History of the Dividing Line, Telephone Books, 1979
Pythagorean Silence, The Montemora Foundation, 1982
Defenestration of Prague, The Kulchur Foundation, 1983
Articulation of Sound Forms in Time, Awede Press, 1987
A Bibliography of the King's Book or, Eikon Basilike, Paradigm Press, 1989
The Europe of Trusts: Selected Poems, Sun & Moon Press, 1990
Singularities, Wesleyan University Press, 1990
The Nonconformist's Memorial, New Directions, 1993

Criticism

My Emily Dickinson, North Atlantic Books, 1985
The Birth-mark: Unsettling the Wilderness in American Literary History, Wesleyan University Press, 1993

The Nonconformist's Memorial

Poems by Susan Howe

A NEW DIRECTIONS BOOK

1993

ACKNOWLEDGMENTS

Some of the poems in this book have appeared in the following magazines: *Avec, American Poetry Review, Conjunctions, Dark Ages Clasp the Daisy Root, The Difficulties, Hambone, How(ever), o.blek, Temblor,* and *Verse.*

A Bibliography of the King's Book or, Eikon Basilike was first published by Paradigm Press, Providence, R.I., in 1989. *The Nonconformist's Memorial* was published by The Grenfell Press, New York, in 1992, in a limited edition with illustrations by Robert Mangold.

Melville's Marginalia is indebted to *Melville's Marginalia,* edited by Wilson Walker Cowen, re-edited by Stephen Orgel, published by Garland Publishing Corporation, New York, 1987. Pages 125–27 in *Melville's Marginalia* are taken almost directly from John Mitchel's "James Clarence Mangan: His Life, Poetry, and Death," in *Poems by James Clarence Mangan; with a Biographical Introduction by John Mitchel,* New York, P. M. Haverty, 1859; Louise I.Guiney's *James Clarence Mangan: His Selected Poems With A Study,* Lamson Wolffe & Co., Norwood, Mass., 1897; and John Desmond Sheridan's *James Clarence Mangan,* Dublin, Talbot Press, 1937.

Manufactured in the United States of America
New Directions Books are printed on acid-free paper.
First published as New Directions Paperbook 755 in 1993
Published simultaneously in Canada by Penguin Books Canada Limited

Library of Congress Cataloging–in–Publication Data

Howe, Susan.
The nonconformist's memorial: poems/by Susan Howe
p. cm.
ISBN 0-8112-1229-7(pbk.)
I. Title.
PS3558. 0893N64 1993
813' .54—dc20 92-38489
CIP

New Directions Books are published for James Laughlin
by New Directions Publishing Corporation,
80 Eighth Avenue, New York 10011

SECOND PRINTING

To David von Schlegell

Contents

I

T U R N I N G

The enthusiast suppresses her tears, crushes her opening thoughts, and—all is changed.

Mary Shelley *Journal*, Feb 7, 1822.

Marked by Herman Melville in his copy of *Shelley Memorials.*

THE NONCONFORMIST'S MEMORIAL

20.15 Jesus saith unto her, Woman,
why weepest thou? whom seekest
thou? She, supposing him to be the
gardener, saith unto him, Sir, if thou
have borne him hence, tell me where
thou has laid him, and I will take
him away.
16 Jesus saith unto her, Mary. She
turned herself, and saith unto him,
Rabboni; which is to say, Master.
17 Jesus saith unto her, Touch me
not; for I am not yet ascended to
my Father: but go to my brethren,
and say unto them, I ascend unto my
Father, and your Father; and *to* my
God, and your God.
18 Mary Magdalene came and told
the disciples that she had seen the
Lord, and *that* he had spoken these
things unto her.

The Gospel According to St. John

Contempt of the world
and contentedness

Lilies at this season

other similitudes
Felicities of life

Preaching constantly
in woods and obscure

dissenting storms
A variety of trials

Revelations had had
and could remember

far away historic fact

Flesh become wheat

which is a nothingness
The I *John* Prologue

Original had no title
Ingrafted onto body

dark night stops suddenly
It is the last time

Run then run run

Often wild ones nest in woods
Every rational being

The act of Uniformity
ejected her
and informers at her heels
Citations remain abbreviated
Often a shortcut
stands for Chapter

1.

nether John and John harbinger

In Peter she is nameless
Actual world nothing ideal

headstrong anarchy thoughts
A single thread of narrative

She was coming to anoint him
As if all history were a progress

As if all history were a progress
She was coming to anoint him
A single thread of narrative
headstrong anarchy thoughts
Actual world nothing ideal

In Peter she is nameless
The nets were not torn

The Gospel did not grasp

Whether the words be a command
words be a command issuing from authority or counsel

Mortal contained in it as

Dissent is gathered in the place

night drift shreds earth knowledge

This writing is understood

having counted the cost

Wind blowing and veering

More in faith as to sense

Testimony

Where he says He

Upon Cherubim

in deep ocean

First anything so later

Must have been astonished

dark background (Gardener

Pure Sacrosanct Negator

I John bright picture

What am I?

suddenly unperceivable time from place to place

All other peace Effectual crucifying knowledge

I John bright picture

dark background (Gardener

Must have been astonished

First anything so later

Testimony

More in faith as to sense

Having counted the cost

his hiding is understood

Mortal contained in it

a state of separation

The soul's ascension in

Where he says He

Upon the Cherubim

Baffled consuming doggerel

and in deep ocean

In the Evangelist's mind
it is I absolutely I
Word before name
Resurrection and life are one
it is I
without any real subject
all that I say is I
A predicate nominative
not subject the I is
the bread the light the door
the way the shepherd the vine

Stoics Academics Peripatetics

and liturgical fierce adversity symbol

Hazard visionary ages foursquare

She ran forward to touch him
Alabaster and confess

Don't cling to me
Pivot

Literally the unmoving point around which a body turns
Literally stop touching me

We plural are the speaker

Came saw went running told
Came along
Solution continuous chaos
Asked told observed
Caught sight of said said
Wrapped lying there
Evangelists refer to dawn
The Three Day Reckoning
Alone in the dark to a place of
execution
Wording of an earlier tradition
Disciples are huddled together
We do not know
The Evangelist from tradition
He bent down
Mary was standing
In the synoptic tradition Mary
enters the tomb

The Narrative of Finding

One solitude lies alone
Can be represented

where the capture breaking
along the shock wave

interpreted as space-time
on a few parameters

Only in the absolute sky
as it is in Itself

word flesh crumbled page edge

The shadow of history
is the ground of faith

A question of overthrowing

Formulae of striking force
Vision and such possession

How could Love not be loved

Disciples are huddled together
They do not know

Retrospective chronologies
Synoptics speak

Revelatory Discourse Source
The Feeding Narrative in Mark

Rough messenger Trust
I studious am

Would never have stumbled
on the paved road

What is that law

You have your names

To do and to settle
Spirit of Conviction

Who wounded the earth

Out of the way of Night
no reason to count

Crying out testimony

Paths of righteousness
Love may be a stumbling

out on the great meadows
Prose is unknown

You have your names

I have not read them

Coming from a remote field
abandoned to me

The motif of fear is missing
The motif of searching

Historicity of the scene
Confused narrative complex

Two women with names
followed by two without names

Distance original disobedience

Against the coldness of force
Intellectual grasp

Scene for what follows
Do not touch me

It is by chance that she weeps
Her weeping is not a lament

She has a voice to cry out

No community can accompany her
No imagination can dream

Improbable disciple passages
Exegetes explain the conflict

Some manuscripts and versions

Her sadness

was out of enclosure

Transfiguration

Out of enclosure She

So many stumble

going out of the world

Come then!

Feet wrapped in hay

I stray to stray

her knowledge of Me

Hearers of the Face Discourse

Happy to be in peace

know next to nothing

She drank a tumbler-full of water

Often singing

Her body trembled like a leaf

2.

19.17 And I saw an angel standing in the sun.
The Revelation of St. John the Divine

Arreption to imagery

of drift meadow edge
of the woods here

Fragility union of glory

What is our defense
Barrier of deafness

aggravated December
Snow and white as wool

bleak bright sea-wind spray

Who will bear witness
What is concupiscence

bare slate-colored cloud

Translate the secret
in lair idiom havoc

What ransom covenant

John was sent as the storm
Word or words together

Sensible as she was
Thought has broken down

Standing in the sun

speaking to Lazarus
this name means Twin

Tell the Corinthians

River meadows
dense dark
Another less dark
Parallelism
As sound is
sense is
in the extreme
who would be Perfect
how disconnectedly
courage fails
this chapter and that
legitimate

Everybody knows but doesn't
how many falls and stumbles
Oh when when

Scene Calvary the open destitute
Under the burden of it
seeking to get to it

Quiet peace

I will use the bare name
Christ

Hallucinated to infinity
as minister of the sea

Walking on the sea and feeding

Intractable ethical paradox

Or break its boundaries
Vindicated by uprightness

Pronoun *I* or her name
utter immensities whisper

nether John and John harbinger
Using we for ourself

In a short lonely human time

some love-impelled figure

Stop clinging to me

He hasn't left the earth

The recognition scene

These are thoughts

This is not intention

as to the sense of it

To be a man of Sorrows

the Person speaking

For there is no Proverb

Here is the depth of it

3.

Immediate Acts

I am not afraid to confess it
and make you my confessor
Steal to a place in the dark
least coherent utterance
and Redactor's treasured proof
Love for the work's sake

Consent in the heavens
Reason in the mind
Walking up and down
Not to be too sudden
As in the case of fasting
alienated
But was a peacemaker
Rebels are quartered here

Arranges and utters
words to themselves
Of how and first she
was possible body
Pamphlets on that side
the author of them
Parallel to the mind
a reprobate mind clings
close
inner outlaw impenitent
Over-againstness at least
Rigorism

As though beside herself
I want to accuse myself
would say to her confessor
Confessions implode into otherness
Lay at night on thorns
For the purpose of self-concealment
would have consumed iron
And she fled her ecstasies
many occasions

The penultimate Redactor
Some love-impelled figure
Most midnightly thesis
impelled will freely led
Love is the orbed circle
Silent the one sought
Reader if I told anything
my crookedness roughness
Down from his arms
as S. John says in Apocalypse

King of Righteousness
At the end of history
interminable trajectory of authority
So truly primitive
Night when the warrant comes
such a ravenous coming
Undertype Shadow Sacrifice
Who is this distance
Waiting for a restoration
and righteousness

On the losing side
No abiding habitation
Severity of the times
escaped by mistake
Settled somewhere
Inner life led by herself
The clear negative way
Moving away into depths
of the sea
Love once said in her mind
Enlightenedly to do

The metaphor of a stake
Arrow thrust through
In connection with here
Eschatology
At deepest claimlessness
could not see one another
Spirit snapping after air
dragged down to visible
Chroniclers halt of such
authentic sayings
Fear destroys all welcome
house-arrest

She fled from consolation
The abiding and transitory
were negative and no echo
These attacks came suddenly
even fierce as the Evangelist
the struggle in S. John
darkness rushing and the true
I will cross the frontiers
Pure hard-edged discipline
betrothes to me nothing
She is matron undone her hair
falling down

Is that the same as Hell
Theologians in that fire
As to her physical health
and the fire
As night to understanding
or truth to fiction
stammering to a redaction
the quick and simplicity
Believing unbelieving reader
there is now no rest
She confessed to a Confessor
tell lies and I will tell

I wander about as an exile
as a body does a shadow
A notion of split reference
if in silence hidden by darkness
there must be a Ghost
Iconic theory of metaphor
a sound and perfect voice
Its hiding is understood
Reader I do not wish to hide
in you to hide from you
It is the Word to whom she turns
True submission and subjection

Were Protestant dissenters
Who walk along this road
Who knows better than you know
I remember the strangers
Not finding names there
Immanence is white with this
Where to find charges
A hymn was contesting a claim
Court of interior recollection
Map of a wilderness of sin
There I cannot find there
I cannot hear your wandering prayer
of quiet

When night came on
Windows to be opened
so as to see the sky
She saw herself bereft
of body
would only seem to sleep
If I could go back
Recollectedly into biblical
fierce grace
already fatherless
Isled on all removes
When night came on

Dense in parameter space
the obscure negative way
Any trajectory is dense
outside the threshold
Turn again and lean against
Moving away into depths
of the sea
Her Love once said in her mind
Enlightenedly to do

SILENCE WAGER STORIES

When I come to view
about steadfastness
Espousal is as ever
Evil never unravels
Memory was and will be
yet mercy flows
Mercies to me and mine
Night rainy my family
in private and family

I know I know short conviction
have losses then let me see why

To what distance and by what path
I thought you would come away

1

Battered out of Isaiah
Prophets stand gazing
Formed from earth
In sure and certain
What can be thought
Who go down to hell alive
is the theme of this work
I walk its broad shield
Every sign by itself
havoc brood from afar
Letting the slip out
Glorious in faithfulness
Reason never thought saw

2

You already have brine
Reason swept all away
Disciples are fishermen
Go to them for direction

Gospel of law Gospel of shadow
in the vale of behavior
who is the transgressor
Far thought for thought
nearer one to the other
I know and do not know
Non attachment dwell on nothing
Peace be in this house
Only his name and truth

3

Having a great way to go
it struck at my life
how you conformed to dust
I have taken the library
Volumes might be written
ambiguous signs by name
Near nightfall it touches it
Nothing can forbear it
So fierce and so flaring
Sometimes by the seaside
all echoes link as air
Not I cannot tell what
so wanton and so all about

4

Fields have vanished
The Mower his hopes
Bow broke time loose
none but my shadow
she to have lived on
with the wood-siege
nesting in this poem
Departed from the body
at home of the story
I'm free and I'm famished
And so to the Irish
Patrol sentinel ensign
Please feel my arms open

5

The issue of legitimation
Identity of the subject
Circumcision of a heart
driven outside its secret
Elysian solitary imagination
by doubt but not by sight
Fear that forever forever
perfect Charity casts out
The Canticle is an allegory
unchangeable but changeable
Fluttering robes of Covetous

He is incomprehensible he
makes darkness his covert

6

Ages pre-supposed ages
the darkness of life
out of necessity night
being a defense by day
the cause and way to it
From same to the same
These joining together
and having allegiance
Words are an illusion
are vibrations of air
Fabricating senselessness
He has shattered gates
thrown open to himself

7

Though lost I love
Love unburied lies
No echo newlyfledge
Thought but thought
the moving cause
the execution of it
Only for theft's sake
even though even

perturb the peace
But for the hate of it
questionless limit
unassuaged newlyfledge
A counter-Covenant

8

Mysterious as night itself
All negligently scenery
if Nothing could be seen
Sacraments are mysterious
Ambiguous in literal meaning
the Pentateuch the Angels John
all men form a silent man
who wrote the author down
Sackcloth itself is humility
a word prerogatives array
Language a wood for thought
over the pantomime of thought
Words words night unto night

9

Drift of human mortality
what is the drift of words
Pure thoughts are coupled
Turn your face to what told me
love grazed here at least

mutinous predominant unapparent
What is unseen is eternal
Judgments are a great deep
Confession comes to nought
half to be taken half left
From communion of wrongdoing
doubleness among the nouns
I feed and feed upon names

10

Claim foreign order
dismantling mortal
Begotten possibility
plummet fetter seem
So coldly systems break
Fraught atvantaging
Two tell againstself
Theme theme heart fury
all in mutiny
Troubleless or sadder
Estranged of all strange
Let my soul quell
Give my soul ease

11

Antic prelate treason
I put on haircloth

Clear unutterable
Secret but tell
What diadem bright
Theme theme heart fury
Winged knowledge hush
Billeted near presage
such themes do quell
Claim foreign order
Plummet fetter seem
wild as loveDeath
Two tell against self

12

Strange fear of sleep
am bafflement gone
Bat winged dim dawn
herthe midmost wide
I did this and I
But forever you say
Bafflement nether elegy
herthe otherwise I
Irreconcilable theme
keep silent then
Strange always strange
Estrange that I desire
Keep cover come cover

13

Lies are stirring storms
I listen spheres from far
Whereunder shoreward away
you walked here Protector
unassuaged asunder thought
you walked here Overshadow
I listen spheres of stars
I draw you close ever so
Communion come down and down
Quiet place to stop here
Who knows ever no one knows
to know unlove no forgive

Half thought thought otherwise
loveless and sleepless the sea
Where you are where I would be
half thought thought otherwise
Loveless and sleepless the sea

II

C O N V E R S I O N

I like to be stationary.

—Bartleby

A BIBLIOGRAPHY OF THE KING'S BOOK OR, EIKON BASILIKE

MAKING THE GHOST WALK ABOUT AGAIN AND AGAIN

On the morning of 30 January 1649, King Charles I of England walked under guard from St. James to Whitehall. At 2 p.m. he stepped from a window of the Banqueting House, out onto the scaffold. He was separated from the large crowd of citizens who had gathered to see his execution by ranks of soldiers so his last speech could only be heard by the attending chaplain and a few others with them on the scaffold.

The King's last word "Remember" was spoken to Bishop Juxon. What Charles meant his chaplain to remember is still a mystery.

Philip Henry witnessed the spectacle. He later wrote: "The blow I saw given; and can truly say with a sad heart, at the instant whereof I remember well, there was such a grone by the Thousands then present as I never heard before and desire I may never hear again."

The gentle and stoic behavior of King Charles I at the scene leading up to his beheading transformed him into a martyr in the eyes of many. His fate was compared to the Crucifixon and his trial to the trial of Jesus by the Romans. Handkerchiefs dipped in his blood were said to bring miracles. On the day of the execution *The Eikon Basilike, The Pourtraicture of His Sacred Majestie in his Solitude and Sufferings,* was published and widely distributed throughout England, despite the best efforts of government censors to get rid of it.

The *Eikon* was supposed to have been written by the King. It consists of essays, explanations, prayers, debates, emblems and justifications of the Royalist cause.

Printers of the *Eikon Basilike* were hunted down and imprisoned. But in spite of many obstacles the little book was set in type time and again.

During 1649 fresh editions appeared almost daily and sold out at once. The *Eikon Basilike*'s popularity continued throughout the years of the Commonwealth and Cromwell's Protectorate.

The *Eikon Basilike* is a forgery.

At the Restoration, John Gauden, a writer who was also a bishop, claimed authorship. He was advanced to the see of Worcester in recognition of this service to the Crown, because Lord Clarendon and Charles II believed him.

King Charles I was a devoted patron of the arts. He particularly admired Shakespeare. His own performance on the scaffold was worthy of that author-actor who played the part of the Ghost in *Hamlet.* The real King's last word "Remember" recalls the fictive Ghost-king's admonition to his son. The ghost of a king certainly haunted the Puritans and the years of the Protectorate. Charles I became the ghost of Hamlet's father, Caesar's ghost, Banquo's ghost, the ghost of King Richard II.

In 1649, two months after the execution, John Milton was awarded the secretaryship for foreign tongues to the council state of the new commonwealth in recognition of his pamphlet, *The Tenure of Kings and Magistrates.*

The *Tenure* is a defense of Regicide.

The chief duties of a Latin Secretary were the drafting and translation of international letters and treaties; Latin was the diplomatic language and was used in diplomatic correspondence. While Walter Frost, the general secretary, conducted most general correspondence, Milton was expected to intellectually bolster the new and struggling civil authority. He examined state papers, investigated and interrogated authors and suspected printers, and as a "diligent . . . partisan, controversialist," composed several crucial political tracts for the Council of State. If Royalists represented the killing of the King, in sermons and pamphets, as a secular rite of passion; Milton argued that Charles had been an ineffectual leader,

> a deep dissembler, not of his affections onely, but of religion. . . . People that should seek a King, claiming what this man claimes, would show themselves to be by nature slaves, and arrant beasts; not fitt for that liberty which they cri'd out and bellow'd for, but fitter to be led back again into their own servitude, like a sort of clamouring & fighting brutes, broke loos from their copyholds.

Charles I had been a threat to true Christians who followed their intellectual consciences as informed by God, instead of performing empty and dogmatic church rituals whose purpose was to support a corrupt state. Milton defended a new rationalism in the violent revolutionary struggle.

Eikon Basilike means the Royal Image. *Eikonoklastes* can be translated "Image Smasher."

One of Milton's chief points of attack on the *Eikon* concerned "A prayer in time of Captivity," said to have been delivered to Bishop Juxon, by

Charles on the scaffold. The prayer, a close paraphrase from "no serious Book, but the vain amatorious Poem of Sr Philip Sidney's *Arcadia*," was the prayer of a pagan woman to an all-seeing heathen Deity.

A captive Shepherdess has entered through a gap in ideology. "Pammela in the Countesses Arcadia," confronts the inauthentic literary work with its beginnings in a breach.

Fictive Pamela's religious supplications were a major issue in the ensuing authorship controversy. Scholars and bibliographers accused Milton of "contrivance" in procuring the insertion of her prayer among the King's last devotions in order to ridicule the authenticity of all the gathered notes and essays. The charge has been confirmed, and denied.

In 1680, an official edition of the *Eikon*, sanctioned by King Charles II, subtracted all the prayers. Other post-Restoration *Basilikas* and *Reliquiae Sacrae*, some dedicated to the new monarch, included the seven prayers with Pamela's leading the file. A great deal of energy and confusion has been expended and expounded since then; by bibliographers, scholars, poets, critics, and other impassioned crusaders, including Samuel Johnson, Christopher Wordsworth, and William Empson, over correctly identifying the first edition to carry the "forged" prayer.

The *Eikon Basilike* is a puzzle. It may be a collection of meditations written by a ghostly king; it may be a forged collection of meditations gathered by a ghostwriter who was a Presbyterian, a bishop, a plagiarizer, and a forger.

Eikonoklastes is a political tract. It was written by the poet-propogandist-author of "L'Allegro," "Il Penseroso," "Comus," and *Areopagitica, a Speech For the Liberty of Unlicenc'd Printing, To the Parliament of England* while he was acting as the Latin Secretary, a government censor, and an image smasher.

But it is *A Bibliography of the King's Book; or, Eikon Basilike*, by Edward Almack, that interests me. My son found it at one of the sales Sterling Memorial Library sometimes holds to get rid of useless books.

Almack's *Bibliography* was published in 1896 in support of Royal authorship. Francis F. Madan's *A New Bibliography of the Eikon Basilike of King Charles the First, with a note on the authorship* was published in 1950 in support of John Gauden. *A New Bibliography* is still in Sterling Library.

Webster's Third International Dictionary says a bibliographer is "one that writes about or is informed about books, their authorship, format, publication, and similar details." Is he or she supposed to compile a set of authoritative texts that can withstand the charge of forgery, the test of time, the timeliness of libraries?

A bibliography is "the history, identification, or analytical and systematic description or classification of writings or publications considered as material objects." Can we ever really discover the original text? Was there ever an original poem? What is a pure text invented by an author? Is such a conception possible? Only by going back to the pre-scriptive level of thought process can "authorial intention" finally be located, and then the material object has become immaterial.

Here is a book called *A Bibliography of the King's Book; or, Eikon Basilike.* Edward Almack meant to describe each material edition, but the vexed question of authorship kept intruding itself.

Pierre Macherey's description of the discourse in a fiction applies to the discourse in this bibliography: "sealed and interminably completed or endlessly beginning again, diffuse and dense, coiled about an absent centre which it can neither conceal nor reveal."

The absent center is the ghost of a king.

Oh Lord
o Lord
different from
Laws
zeal
transposed
OMne
envions
obwructions
bearing

comand

nfortunate Mans

un ust
woule
Futnre
audPaged doe of Title-page

No further trace
of the printer

IN | HIS | SOLITUDE | To The
Reader the work

Prayers, &c. belonging
to no one without
Reasons

And in a stage play all the people know right wel, that he that playeth the sowdayne is percase a sowter. Yet if one should can so lyttle good, to shewe out of seasonne what acquaintance he hath with him and calle him by his owne name whyle he standeth in his magestie, one of his tormenters might hap to breake his head, and worthy for marring of the play. And so they said that these matters bee Kynges games, as it were stage playes, and for the most part plaied upon scafoldes, in which pore men be but ye lokers-on. And they; yt wise be, wil medle no farther. For they that sometyme step vp and play wt them, when they cannot play their partes, they disorder the play & do themself no good.

The History of King Richard The Third (unfinished), Sir Thomas More

ΕΙΚΩΝ ΒΑΣΙΛΙΚΗ.

Steps between Prison and Grave Brazen Wall I

Bradshaw went on in a long harangue misapplying Law and History

Language of state secrets

The pretended Court
of Justiice

Upon the picture of His Majesty sitting in his Chair | before

the High Court of Injustice

Small trespas to misprison

now nonexistent dramatis personae
confront each
other

Heroic Virtue & Fame

ENGELANDTS MEMORIAEL

Tragicum Theatrum Actorum

Similar (not identical)

unsigned portraits of

Laud Charles I Fairfax

Holland Hamilton Capel

Cromwell

crucified by Ordinance
That sea of blood

The malicious author or instigator Forts Navy Militia
Tract the treasons
throw down
message
Always causes set down
an intellectualist
for a different message
of Joy
O make me
Some passages
thrown on this person
Was taken
Through populacy
through the populacy
A
p v o t
Contemporary History
The People
in a low voice
two or three words
He bowed down his head and said
they kept
pas

that I hide Security and their
Security

and wall the brazen wall

P r i s o n s
I am weary of life
Pretend Justice to cover Perjury
between
s p e t s

strive against starry scruples
at times at times

The sentiment sentiment
Goes peers ferrets to the last

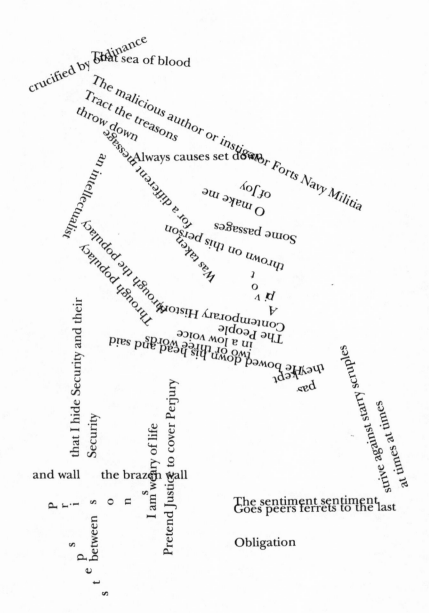

Obligation

P r i s o n s

s t e p s

between

and wall

that I hide Security and their

Security

the brazen wall

I am weary of life

Pretend Justice to cover Perjury

Obligation

The sentiment sentiment

Goes peers ferrets to the last

strive against starry scruples

at times at times

pas-

they kept

He bowed down his head and said

two or three words

in a low voice

The People

Contemporary History

A pivot

Through populacy

through the populacy

Was taken

for a different message

thrown on this person

Some passages

O make me

of Joy

an intellectualist

Always causes set down

The malicious author or instigator Forts Navy Militia

Tract the treasons

throw down

crucified by that sea of blood

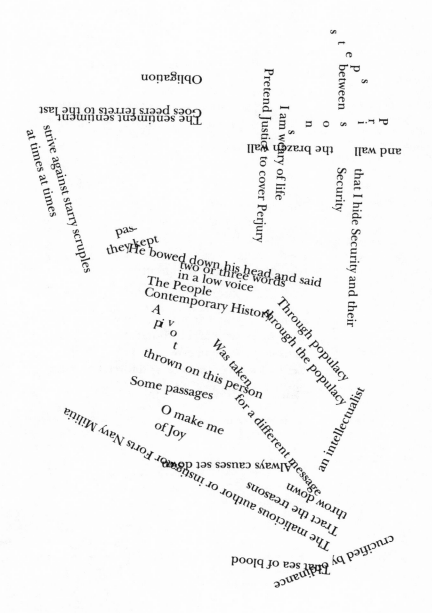

Ordinance

Finding the way full of People
Who had placed themselves upon the Theatre
To behold the Tragedy
He desired he might have *Room*
to the right
Speech came from his mouth
Historiography of open fields
Signed W. King in profile

Mend the Printers faults
T
The place name and field name
as thou doest them espy
Centuries of compulsion and forced holding
For the Author lies in Gaol
All the Civil War Authorities

and knows not why

A cleric's forgery
of a pseudo-biographical
apology

England's Black Tribunal : Containing The Complete Tryal of King CHARLES the First, by the pretended High Court of Justice in *Westminster-Hall*, begun *Jan.* 20, 1648. Together with His Majesty's Speech on the Scaffold, erected at *Whitehall-Gate*, on Tuesday, *Jan.* 30, 1648.

An intellectualist out of submissive levelling love

His writings
It passed with the Negative.
they kept prisoner
He bowed down his head and said
two or three words
in a low voice
The People
Contemporary History
A
pivot
Was taken
through the populacy
Through populacy
thrown on this person
Some passages
for a different message
intellectualist
O make me
of Joy

Dr. Juxon. There is but one Stage more, this Stage is turbulent and troublesome, it is a short one; but you may consider, it will soon carry you a very great Way: It will carry you from Earth to Heaven, and there you shall find a great deal of cordial Joy and Comfort.

King. I go from a corruptible to an incorruptible Crown, where no Disturbance can be, no Disturbance in the World

This still house

An unbeaten way

My self and words

The King kneeling

Old raggs about him

All those apopthegems

Civil and Sacred

torn among fragments

Emblems gold and lead

Must lie outside the house
Side of space I must cross

To write against the Ghost

Bibliography Of The Authorship Controversy

STay Passenger

BE*hold* a Mirror

A First didn't write it

Anguish of the heart
Smart of the cure

Strip furlong field

Feet on someone else's wheat

Easy market access

On-going struggle
abandoned lands

Lost power of expression
Last power of expression

The Battle of Corioli

Obsessive images of Coriolanus

The Author and Finisher
The Author of the Fact

of Gold of Thorn of Glory

Driest facts
of bibliography
Scarce tract work
pagination signatures running
The borrower
Stamp of the King's
own character
I am a seeker
Blades Blades & Blades

Tell you my author
I knew his hand
The book was his
The cloathing *Hands*
I am a seeker
of water-marks
in the Antiquity
The Sovereign stile
in another stile
Left scattered in disguise

No men
as expected
ever will be
Saviors
Curtain the background
in the cropping cycle
within the bounds

This word *Remember*
The army and their
abettors
after the murder
of the King
Forever our Solomon
Sent forth into
a Christian world
He is speaking
to the army

Great Caesar's ghost
Through history
this is the counter-plot
and turns our swords in
The First Revolution
The Foundation of hearsay
Horrifying drift errancy
A form and nearby form

In his sister's papers
they often had discourse
The King was trusting
the Kingdom brambles
Printing an edition
of the *Eikon Basilike*
Insertion of prayer
from Sidney's *Arcadia*
The *Eikon* is an imposture
True image antic sun
Amateur such as the King
Saying so I name nobody

Heathen woman
out of heathen legend
in a little scrip
the First's own hand
Counterfeit piece
published to undeceive
the world
In his reply Pseudomisus
shifts the balance
of emphasis

Et Chaos & Phlegethon
Mrs Gauden's Nar-/
rative
attributed in Primitive
times to Jesus Christ
his Apostles and other
papers Regicides took
The Dutch Narrative
and Perrinchief's *Life*
Harsnett's *Declaration*
is a weapon

C * R and skull on covers
MADESTIE
More than Conqueror, &c.
King on the binding
1 blank leaf
The lip of truth
A lying tongue
Great Caesar's ghost
She is the blank page
writing ghost writing

Real author of The Lie
"The Lie" itself
fallible unavailable
Thin king the Personator
in his absolute state
Absolutist identity
Imago Regis Caroli
Falconer Madan's copy
the Truth a truth
Dread catchword THE
the king exactly half-face

Face toward the Court Silence

Scope of the body politic
Mock alphabet and map

Daniel's way was to strew ashes
Ashes strewn on his path

Daniel's way Daniel's way
Archaic Arachne Ariadne

She is gone she sends her memory

In the hall Justice Justice
Parable embedded gospel

upheaved among remembrance
Unfinished four last things

Blunt to a wild of nothing
face the Face of the Court

Truth is property and lie theft

Lesser marginal writers

Unutterable gathering darkness
Fragmentary narrative enclaves

Metaphor of a sea raging
Stormy frontispiece
and striking capital D
Threat cord flung
undone in Chalk Country
Oak cleft to splinters
storm in the Storm itself
Turned to watch Wrath
Eating our bread heads
we wonder under water

Even after the monarchomachists
The regicide hack
Robert Robins
piled up syllogisms

Opening words of *Patriarcha*
Sentences in characters
Judges and ghostly fathers

The first during his captivity
Omitting the *Life*

almost hissing his regality
off the stage Untruth

SALMASIUS. His Dissection
and confutation
of the diabolical rebel
Milton's book *Eikonoklastes*
So bewitched by him
I am afraid of him

View of magisterial authority
Sound of the hammering

Mask visor disguised Representer

To walk side by side with
this chapter was Tumult

sacrosanct veils liturgies

First defender of Regicide
Any authority all authority

In Darkness School Distinction

of one fact for one fact
What is salvaged saved

exempted that falls Protector

form of figure of thought
Came petitioning to levellers

People under the scaffold

Refusing to be on the scaffold

Vast space where restless
half-forgotten migrations

Even the kings of Judah failed

The large cloud breaks open
Style of the Regicide tracts

Fanatical swift moving authority

Thirsty after fame s u o
in the very Eikonoklastes l e
he was the author i f Engk
Pe r p Bruteraher a

Impartial Scout
Mercurius Politicus
Melancholicus

This proclamation, beginning 'Charles R.| Whereas John Milton' is dated Whitehall, 13 August 1660; the text is mostly in black letter. Milton described as 'late of Westminster', is said to be in hiding to avoid trial; the three books are to be handed in, or else seized and publicly burnt, and never to be reprinted. The last line of para. 2 of the text begins 'brought to Legal Tryal'. This edition is Steele 3239. with coat of arms, no. 67, measuring 1 15/16 x 1 11/16 in. And three other copies. Bodl.

Who is not a wild Enthusiast

in a green meadow

furious and fell

Arriving on the stage of history
I saw madness of the world

Stripped of falsification
and corruption

anthems were singing
in Authorem

Father and the Father
by my words will I be justified

Autobiography I saw

Legal righteousness makes us servants
All good hearers

Opposers or despisers
Night page torn word missing

The family silence
gave up the ghost

I feared the fall of my child

resting quietly with some hopes

as a bird before any

Election–Vocation–
Justification–
Cape of Wind wreathe
fame out laughing
Seated on a cloud
Seacret drift
seacretly behest
the dear She
comes to all Guilty
all circling
Eye window soul body
Pride cannot bow
Ariadne's diadem
zodiac helmet belt

A poet's iconoclasm
A bestiary of the Night

I am at home in the library
I will lie down to sleep

A great happy century
A little space among herds

In the High Quire

We that are distant

Paul also was Romans 7

and Ezekial 36 I will take away
the stony heart

C

in the ace of speechstone
Spelling surname

intent
ithuriel

Maii printed so
second i falls below
the line
Maii dropping below
the line

"I Become Friendly With Mr. Dick"

"'Do you recollect the date,' said Mr. Dick, looking earnestly at me, and taking up his pen to note it down, 'when King Charles the First had his head cut off?'

I said I believed it happened in the year sixteen hundred and forty-nine.

"'Well.' returned Mr. Dick, scratching his ear with his pen, and looking dubiously at me. 'So the books say; but . . . if it was so long ago, how could the people about him have made that mistake of putting some of the trouble out of *his* head, after it was taken off, into *mine*?'"

He was sequestered pursevanted plundered in [illegible] after sheet O
Upon authority and extreme rabble cudgel time of Rebellion
His own peculiar spelling founded on the Scottish pronunciation
aftershock of iconoclasm in *Leviathan* So falls that stately | Cedar
18th in Wagstaff's first list
Aftershock of iconoclasm

utmost

light

mote

Spir e

Therfrom
evry
edge

all

Illimited

Ariadne

led Theseus

in every

let down

perceptive

Minos' from
daughter Thread

Sphere

pierced
Light symbolism

Thought Trace
weft

daughter
SWADLIER Centuries I No
rhid
To her Face
Fire
CLOATHE
fate
distant
the lay
Island place
deathless
Place they stood on
Stars
away who remember
Flood Crown
she wore
and the sea
Eyes up

to
Fire

Dominant ideologies drift
Charles I who is "Caesar"
Restless Cromwell who is "Caesar"
Disembodied beyond language
in those copies are copies

K CHARL I WORKS I VOL I
K CHARLE I WORKS I VOL II
Numbers of Prayers, 3.
pp. 1 – 102 ending "FINIS"
It has remains of light blue silk
strings

I was going away, when he directed my attention to the kite.

'What do you think of that for a kite?' he said.

I answered that it was a beautiful one. I should think it must have been as much as seven feet high.

'I made it. We'll go and fly it, you and I,' said Mr. Dick. 'Do you see this?'

He showed me that it was covered with manuscript, very closely and laboriously written; but so plainly, that as I looked along the lines, I thought I saw some allusion to King Charles the First's head again, in one or two places.

'There's plenty of string,' said Mr. Dick, 'and when it flies high, it takes the facts a long way. That's my manner of diffusing 'em. I don't know where they may come down. It's according to circumstances, and the wind, and so forth; but I take my chance of that.'

The Personal History of David Copperfield, Charles Dickens

Silk

symbolic

Praeparative

faith

Ariagne

Idman satter

the set Penned

stars

ARACHNE SUN'S

deft ray

through

She shiel

was Thrieeald

winding trace

wool weft

Cloud

soft

threada

twist

MELVILLE'S MARGINALIA

March 20, 1639-40—
buried Philip Massinger
a stranger.

PARENTHESIS

BRIEF CHRONOLOGY OF JAMES CLARENCE MANGAN

1803 May 1st. Born on Fishamble Street, Dublin. Second son of a schoolteacher turned grocer. His mother had inherited a grocery store. His baptismal name is James. "Clarence" is his later addition.

1810 Enters school in Saul's Court. Is taught some Latin, French, Italian, and Spanish by Father Graham.

1812 [Percy Bysshe Shelley speaks at a meeting 28 February at Fishamble Street and publishes an *Address to the Irish People.* He and Harriet distribute the pamphlets in Dublin. The *Address* is advertised with a summary in *The Dublin Evening Post,* 25, 29 February and again March 3rd.]

1818 Father is bankrupt. Becomes family breadwinner. Is sent to work as a scrivener at Kenrick's, a lawyer's office.

1818-26 Writes rhyming puzzles for *Jones Diary, Grant's Almanack,* and the *New Ladies Almanack.* Poems begin appearing in almanacs under various pseudonyms: "Peter Puff," "M.E.," "P.V. McGuffin," etc.

1825 Kenrick's closes. Employed as a scrivener for Franks and Leland.

1829 [Catholic Emancipation Act.]

1831 Member of the Comet Club fighting the levying of tithes for Protestant clergy, many of them absentees. By this time is addicted to alcohol, and possibly opium. Adopts the middle name Clarence.

1832-33 Contributor to *The Comet,* the Club's reform newspaper, until its closure by Crown prosecution. Teaches Catherine Hayes German until her death. Writes "Elegaic Verses on Death of a Beloved Friend."

1834-49 Contributes translations of German poetry to the *Dublin University Magazine* : also "translations" from Arabic, Turkish, and Persian. Contributes translations and philosophical poems to the *Dublin Penny Journal* begun by George Petrie and Caesar Otway in 1832.

1838 Becomes a copier for Irish Ordnance Survey; serves as a copyist and transcriber of documents under George Petrie, John O'Donovan, and Eugene O'Curry, scholar-antiquarians responsible for establishing English forms for Gaelic place names for the first Irish Six-Inch-Survey Map. The director, Thomas Larcom, extends the survey to include Irish folklore, nomenclature, and architecture. Project discontinued in 1841.

1841 Two papers on "German Ghosts and Ghost Seers" by "Irys Herfner" (anagram for Henry Ferris) are at first thought to be by Mangan. Starts to disappear from society and return after long absences.

1842 First issue of *The Nation,* the organ of the Young Ireland Movement, founded by Charles Gavan Duffy, Thomas Davis, and John Blake Dillon; includes Mangan's poems, sometimes under the names "Vacuus" and "Terrae Filis," although his work for the magazine isn't overtly political or nationalistic.

1843 Death of James Mangan, James Clarence's father.

1844 Assistant cataloguer at Trinity College Library. Composes or translates "The Karamanian Exile" and other Ottoman poetry.

1845 *Anthologia Germanica* —only volume of work published in his lifetime. Duffy finances the project.

1845-1849 The Irish Famine.

1846 Death of Catherine Smith (Mangan's mother).

1846-49 "Dark Rosaleen," "A Vision of Connaught in the Thirteenth Century," and "The Warning Voice" appear in *The Nation.*

1848 *United Irishman* founded. John Mitchel, its editor, is transported for sedition. Abortive rising of a section of the Young Ireland Movement. One story says that Mangan's association with the group leads to his dismissal from Trinity College Library; another says the poet refused to shave off his mustache when all clerks were required to be unshaven.

1849 Writes "Fragment of an Unfinished Autobiography" for his friend and confessor Father C.P. Meehan. Father Meehan, a nationalist, contributes to *The Nation* under the pen name "Clericus." A quotation from Philip Massinger opens "Fragment of an Unfinished Autobiography": ". . . A heavy shadow lay/On that boy's spirit: he was not of his fathers."

1849 Dies in the Meath Hospital, Dublin, June 20, probably from starvation.

1853 At sunrise on November 8, 1853, there appears, suddenly as Manco Capac at the lake Titicaca, a figure, pallidly neat, pitiably respectable, incurably forlorn, in *Putnam's Monthly Magazine* in New York City. It is Bartleby.

PREFACE

But I have swam through libraries.

Moby-Dick; or The Whale.

After the critical and public failure of *Moby-Dick* and then *Pierre* in 1851-53 Herman Melville became increasingly isolated from his peers. His life was reading and writing. His friends were the philosophers, poets, dramatists, novelists, historians, biographers, critics, journalists, writers of guide books, tracts, narratives, memoirs, and letters, whose works he read. Melville read with a pencil in his hand. Marks he made in the margins of his books are often a conversation with the dead.

> Went to Baths of Caracalla —Wonderful. Massive. Ruins form, as it were, natural bridges of thousands of arches. There are glades, & thickets among the ruins—high up. —Thought of Shelley. Truly, he got his inspiration here. Corresponds with his drama & mind. Still majestic, & desolate grandure. —After much trouble & sore travel without a guide managed to get to Protestant Burial Ground & pyramid of Cestius under walls. Read Keats' epitaph. Separated from the adjacent ground by trench.—Shelley in other ground. Plain stone.— (Went from Caracalla to Shelley's grave by natural process) Thence to Cenci Palace.
>
> Melville's *Journal.* Friday February 27th, 1857.

During the spring of 1991 I was teaching *Billy Budd* for a graduate seminar in Philadelphia. One day while searching through Melville criticism at the Temple University Library I noticed two maroon dictionary-size volumes, lying haphazardly, out of reach, almost out of sight on the topmost shelf. That's how I found *Melville's Marginalia* or *Melville's Marginalia* found me.

* * *

I built a cottage for Susan and myself and made a gateway in the form of a Gothic Arch, by setting up a whale's jaw bones.

Hawthorne's *Twice Told Tales*, Melville's *Moby-Dick* "Extracts," and *Melville's Marginalia*.

Wilson Walker Cowen, using Merton Sealt's checklist (*Harvard Library Bulletin* 1948-50) as a guide, collected and transcribed every page from every known volume of Herman Melville's library that Melville had marked or annotated. Only the pages Melville marked in each book are included so there is little forward trajectory to whatever novel, narrative, or poem. Each marked passage is a literal transcription from the particular edition Melville used. Because Cowen used each original's type-set line-lengths, prose often looks like poetry. Texts in the *Marginalia* are alphabetically arranged by an author's name so authors and writers meet by letter. Cowen submitted this synthesis of attraction and withdrawal to "The Department of English in partial fulfillment of the requirements for the degree of Doctor of Philosophy in the subject of English, Harvard University, Cambridge, Massachusetts, June, 1965."

Scholarly investigators have consulted and are still consulting Melville's marginal notations. The notations and annotations have been marshalled to support one critical reading or another. Wilson Walker Cowen's approach is loving. His informative and detailed introduction shows us why this author's marks seem to indicate agreement with what he was reading; when Melville disagreed he argued in the margin.

Some marginal notes in Melville's books have been erased by someone. The erasures puzzle Cowen. Much of the erased material concerns Melville's feelings and reactions to women. Cowen does have opinions here. He says that since Melville spent a lifetime thinking about women, even though they seldom appear in his fiction, the misogynous nature of the nearly obliterated markings shows the author was much too disturbed by this subject to write about it.

Still—before leaving the persistent problem of eradication in the marginal body of his subject matter Wilson Walker Cowen meditates on the provenance of the corruption.

Elizabeth Shaw Melville is probably the culprit.

She is the Perpetrator-With-Eraser.

"There is no question but that she examined at least some of her husband's books and possessed the opportunity after his death to alter them if she wished. Her scrupulosity in signing her own annotations does not eliminate the possibility that she may have done some other editing. Indeed, it may be an effort to disguise her part in actions of that sort." Cowen is bound to admit some of the rubbing out seems to have been done hastily by a person unfamiliar with Melville's methods of annotation. "If the books were erased by later hands it appears more likely to have been Melville's daughters, Elizabeth and Frances, than Mrs. Osborne and Mrs. Metcalf who have generously made Melville's library available to scholars."

Margins speak of fringes of consciousness or marginal associations.
What is the shadow reflex of art I am in the margins of doubt.

In 1987, as if to emphasize the difference between dissertations and books or between graduate students and professors, the title page of *Melville's Marginalia* reads: "*Harvard Dissertations in American and English Literature,* Edited by Stephen Orgel, Stanford University, A Garland Series:" Wilson Walker Cowen's name and the name of his work follow on page two.

The extracts in *Melville's Marginalia* were collected, transcribed, and collated by a dedicated sub-sub-graduate student in a time before librarians, scholars, and authors relied on computers or Xerox machines. Perhaps his leviathan-dissertation exhausted him. The copyright page of the Garland edition lists Melville's dates, 1819-91 and the dates of Cowen, 1934-87.

Mrs. Wilson Walker Cowen holds the copyright to his recently resurrected body of work.

Stephen Orgel's edited reprint is currently out of print.

Wilson Walker Cowen was a burrower whose commentator I am.

Sometimes I wonder if Mrs. Wilson Walker Cowen is Wilson Walker's widow or his mother.

* * *

This is a long letter, but you are not at all bound to answer it. Possibly, if you do answer it, and direct it to Herman Melville, you will missend it—for the very fingers that now guide this pen are not precisely the same that just took it up and put it on this paper. Lord, when shall we be done changing? Ah! It's a long stage, and no inn in sight, and night coming, and the body cold. But with you for a passenger, I am content and can be happy. I shall leave the world, I feel, with more satisfaction for having come to know you. Knowing you persuades me more than the Bible of our immortality.

Herman Melville to Nathaniel Hawthorne, November 1851.

Names who are strangers out of bounds of the bound margin: I thought one way to write about a loved author would be to follow what trails he follows through words of others: what if these penciled single double and triple scorings arrows short phrases angry outbursts crosses cryptic ciphers sudden enthusiasms mysterious erasures have come to find you too, here again, now.

Round about the margin or edge of anything in a way that is close to the limit. A narrow margin. Slightly.

If water is margined-imagined by the tender grass.

Marginal. Belonging to the brink or margent.

The brink or brim of anything from telepathy to poetry.

A marginal growth of willow and water flag.

A feather on the edge of a bird's wing.

August 1992

Bats on my wing suggest tatters

Let me in my fellow creatures

1.

One anecdote I may be permitted to give here, which will somewhat illustrate the peculiar condition of my moral and intellectual being at this period. I had been sent to Mr. Courtney's Academy in Derby Square. [*Should be Saul's Court.*] It was the first evening of my entrance (in 1820), when I had completed my eleventh year. [*This is a palpable error, for he was born in 1803.*] Twenty boys were arranged in a class; and to me, as the latest comer, was alloted the lowest place—a place with which I was perfectly contented. The question propounded by the schoolmaster was, "What is a parenthesis?" But in vain did he test their philological capacities; one alone attempted some blundering explanation from the grammar; and finally to me, as the forlorn hope that might possibly save the credit of the school, was the query referred. "Sir," said I, "I have only come into the school to-day, and have not had time to look into the grammar; but I should suppose a parenthesis to be something included in a sentence, but which might be omitted from the sentence without injury to the meaning of the sentence." "Go up, sir," exclaimed the master, "to the head of the class." With an emotion of boyish pride I assumed the place allotted me; but the next minute found me once more in my original position. "Why do you go down again, sir?" asked the worthy pedagogue. "Because, sir," cried I, boldly, "I have not deserved the head place; give it to this boy"—and I pointed to the lad who had all but succeeded—"he merits it better, because at least he has tried to study his task." The schoolmaster smiled: he and the usher whispered together, and I was remanded to a seat apart.

James Clarence Mangan, "Fragment Of An Unfinished Autobiography," in *The Poems and Poetry of Ireland* (undated 1883?). Insertions in brackets are footnotes to "Fragment" by C. P. Meehan, C. C. Editor.

A

poet

does not relate

real

events

2. For then

she would clash

with the histo -

rian

connecting

them

by a verbal

association

in a strange

order

Crumple

and stammer out difficulty

Almost

Forced

Loans

. . . A song supposed to be sung by a migratory gang of Thugs from India, lies before us. Fortunately it is of questionable authenticity . . .

Footnote by James Clarence Mangan to his "translation" of "The Thug's Ditty" in *The Dubliner: The Lives, Times and Writings of James Clarence Mangan* by Brendan Clifford. 1988.

[I found I had not taken the first two lines of the first verse. When I went to get them, the British Museum had withdrawn the *Dublin University Magazine* for re-binding. Since the writing of Irish history is possible only because of the care with which the British Museum has preserved Irish materials one can hardly complain when that care becomes an obstacle]

Brendan Clifford's editorial comment to "The Thug's Ditty."

THE MANNER OF LIVING
WITH
and birthright to insult me
GREAT MEN
Led I used not to see
take it to be their privilege
xwhat delicate irony

Life deceives us
Whose life was spent
naturally
in going from one house
Magnanimity cannot
to another
Those who have been wronged
now in literature

One evening in my attic when Maegher in presence of D.F. MacCarthy, R.D. Williams, and half a dozen more, was reciting Antony's oration, over Caesar's corpse, and came to the "lend me your ears"—Mangan stood up gravely and said, "That's a wrong reading." "No," replied the reciter, "it's so in the book." "No matter, sir," rejoined Mangan, "the correct reading is, 'lend me your *cars*,' for Julius was killed near a car-stand, and Antony wanted to get up a decent funeral. What could be more absurd than to ask for a loan of their ears?"

James Meehan's footnote to the Preface of the undated [1883?] Third Edition of *The Poets and Poetry of Munster: A Selection of Irish Songs by the Poets of the Last Century with Poetical Translations by the Late James Clarence Mangan*

Magnanimity cannot
in going from one house

naturally
Whose life was spent

Life deceives us

xwhat delicate irony

take it to be their privilege
Led I used not to see
GREAT MEN
and birthright to insult me

WITH

THE MANNER OF LIVING
The bark of parchment

NONCOMPATIBLES

So baneful
He could not storm the alphabet of art
bête x[Bestial ?]
and social weakness
A style so bent on effect and the expense of soul
so far from classic truth and grace
must surely be said to have the note of
PROVINCIALITY

At this time we—that is, my father, my mother, my brothers, my sister, and myself—tenanted one of the dismalest domiciles, perhaps, to be met with in the most forlorn recesses of any city in Europe. It consisted of two wretched rooms, or rather holes, at the rear of a tottering old fragment of a house, or, if the reader please, hovel, in Chancery Lane. [*This is purely imaginary; and when I told Mangan that I did not think it a faithful picture, he told me he dreamt it.*]

James Clarence Mangan "Autobiography." Insertion in brackets is James Meehan's editorial comment.

SIMPLETONS

Marginal continue?

Must be fall or swerve

must be block or wedge

ADEQUATE EXPRESSION

Re-
venge is
honorable

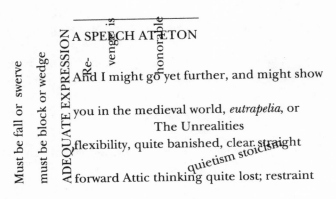

A SPEECH AT ETON

And I might go yet further, and might show

you in the medieval world, *eutrapelia*, or

The Unrealities

flexibility, quite banished, clear. straight

quietism stoicism

forward Attic thinking quite lost; restraint

The Field Imaginary in American Studies

stoppage, and prejudice regnant!

It is pleasant to think of the small blonde sprite of 1811 tripping in and out of the Derby Square school, who may have looked, more than once unawares, on Shelley's boyish self as he went crusading through the streets with Harriet.

Louise I. Guiney, "James Clarence Mangan, A Study," 1897.

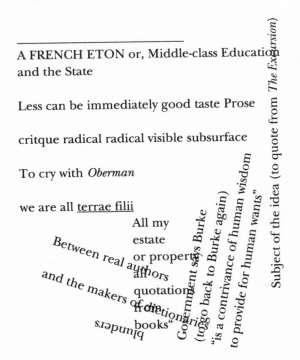

A FRENCH ETON or, Middle-class Education and the State

Less can be immediately good taste Prose

critque radical radical visible subsurface

To cry with *Oberman*

we are all <u>terrae filii</u>

All my
estate
or property
all
quotations
from
books"

Between real authors
and the makers of dictionaries

blunders

Government says Burke
(to go back to Burke again)
"is a contrivance of human wisdom
to provide for human wants"

Subject of the idea (to quote from *The Excursion*)

And the dress of this spectral-looking man was singularly remarkable, taken down at haphazard from some peg in an old clothes shop—a baggy pantaloon that was intended for him, a short coat closely buttoned, a blue cloth cloak still shorter, and tucked so tightly to his person that no one could see there even the faintest shadow of those lines called by painters and sculptors drapery. The hat was in keeping with this habiliment, broad-leafed and steeple-shaped, the model of which he must have found in some picture of Hudibras. Occasionally he substituted for this head-gear, a soldier's fatigue cap, and never appeared abroad in sunshine or storm without a large malformed umbrella, which, when partly covered by the cloak, might easily be mistaken for a Scotch bagpipe.

From C.P. Meehan's Preface to the undated Third Edition of *The Poets and Poetry of Ireland.*

I am sprighted to o

my fo ol is here

Father Meehan tells an interesting story of his first meeting with Mangan. The poet, on being introduced, ran his hands through the priest's hair, and examined his cranial bumps. "Whether he discovered anything to my or to his advantage I do not remember," comments Father Meehan.

It was a strange business. Mangan was both shy and mannerly, and it is not easy to imagine his taking so unwarranted liberty with a head so soon after having been introduced to its owner.

From Louise I. Guiney's "James Clarence Mangan, A Study."

crooked employment?

VERBAL PHANTOMS

Fatally losing and miracle-mongering
as if he were asleep
Whose unique grave
Churchyard road to the grave disappears forever
Mean by fatuity
Writers in these publications
GOETHE calls Halt
employment
The pure lines of an Ionian horizon
The liquid clearness of an Ionian sky
Mean by fatuity
Arnold, Matthew. Essays in Criticism
charm
without
Effective without charm
Boston, Ticknor and Fields, 1865.
Rapidity

John Savage, a contemporary, has left us this picture of him: "He is of middle height, and glides rather than walks. A dark, threadbare coat, buttoned up to the throat, sheathes his attenuated body. His eye is lustrously mild and beautifully blue, and his silver-white locks surround, like a tender halo, the once beautiful and now pale and intellectual face."

W.F. Wakeman, a colleague in the Survey Office, adds some detail, "His teeth were an ill-fitting set, as evidenced by the fact that the wearer was for ever fixing them with his fingers lest they should fall from his gums. He used a large pair of green spectacles. He had narrow shoulders, so much so that for appearance' sake the breast of his coat was thickly padded. His voice was low and sweet, but very tremulous. Sometimes, even in the most settled weather, he might be seen parading the streets with a very voluminous umbrella under each arm."

James Clarence Mangan by John Desmond Sheridan. 1937.

SAYING OF NEDSCHATI.
OB. 1508.
(FROM THE OTTOMAN.)

The world is one vast caravanserai,
Where none may stay,
But where each guest writes on the wall this word,
O MIGHTY LORD! [1]

1. Throughout the East it is the custom for dervishes and other guests, when entering an inn or a monastery, to pencil upon the walls of their apartments a short verse in honor of their entertainer. "O Mighty Lord" is a well-known phrase in the East, expressive of complete subjection and submission. —Mangan's footnote.

Poems of James Clarence Mangan (Many hitherto uncollected) Centenary edition, edited with Preface and Notes by D.J. O'Donoghue. 1903.

I resign to that eternity which is rapidly coming alike upon me, my friends, and my enemies. These latter I also have, and from my heart I say, "May GOD [*Mangan, throughout writes the name of God in capital letters.*] bless them here and hereafter."

"Fragments From An Unfinished Autobiography." Father Meehan's editorial insertion in brackets.

COUNSEL OF A COSMOPOLITAN

p.154—From a very obscure periodical called the *Irish Monthly Magazine*, of October, 1845.

A FAST KEEPER

p. 306—From the *Comet*, 17th March, 1833.

THE WAYFARING TREE

p.308—From the same [DUM], 1845, given as a translation from Selber.

WHERE'S MY MONEY?

p.311—From the *Dublin University Magazine* for 1845.

THE LAUGHTERS

La Bruyère *Works*
harden

into
La Bruyère, Jean de. The Works
ridicule

of M. De la Bruyère. In Two

Name
Volumes. The Which is Added

utterly
the Characters of Theophrastus.

forgot
Also the Manner of Living with
DESTINY
he costs nobody

THE LARK WITH HER YOUNG ONES, WITH THE OWNER OF A FIELD

False news
WHY SHOULD MEN
be blamed
What edits

If you step forward to meet him,   he

Your surprise, Reader, is, doubtless, excited—ah! you know not what a vagabond I am! Perhaps I may communicate my history to the Irish people, and if I should have no hesitation in assuring them that they will pronounce it without a parallel in the Annals of the Marvellous and Mournful. Only see the result!—for me there is no stopping place in city or country. An unrelenting doom condemns me to the incessant exercise of my pedestrian capabilities. It is an awful thing to behold me at each completion of my term scampering off like Van Woedenblock of the Magic Leg—galloping along roads—clearing ditches—dispersing the affrighted poultry in farm yards as effectually as a forty-eight pounder could. Other men sojourn for life in the country of their choice; there is a prospect of ultimate repose for most things; even the March of Intellect must one day halt; already we see that pens, ink, and paper are—stationary.

James Clarence Mangan, "My Bugle, and How I Blow It." *Prose Writings of James Clarence Mangan*, ed. D.J. O'Donoghue, 1904.

M e l v i l l e ' s   M a r g i n a l i a

Secret footsteps cannot bring him

I began to write *Melville's Marginalia* by pulling a phrase, sometimes just a word or a name, at random from Cowen's alphabetically arranged *Melville's Marginalia* and letting that lead me by free association to each separate poem in the series.

Poetry is thought transference.

Free association isn't free.

Finally I spent a week in Cambridge at the Houghton Library examining some of the real books. I saw his large-print volumes of Shakespeare (apparently Melville liked *Cymbeline* nearly as well as *Lear*). I saw *The New Testament with Psalms, Mosses from an Old Manse, Twice-told Tales, Shelley Memorials, The Poetical Works of Andrew Marvell with a Memoir of the Author* ("Starry Vere" written on the back fly-leaf), Schopenhauer's *The World as Will and Idea,* and *Counsels and Maxims,* Emerson's *Essays: Second Series* (furious marginal contradictions in "The Poet"), the heavily marked copies of Matthew Arnold's *Essays in Criticism, Culture and Anarchy,* and *New Poems.*

If there are things Melville went looking for in books so too there were things I looked for in Melville's looking.

Why was I drawn to Mangan?

Only that I remembered the song called "Roisin Dubh" from childhood and my great-aunt's garden one summer years ago beside Killiney Bay near Dublin.

Many people have noted Melville's readings of eminent men: Homer, Dante, Shakespeare, Milton, Marvell, Balzac, Byron, Goethe, Emerson, Hawthorne, Schopenhauer, as well as histories and narratives—Southey's *Life of Nelson,* Moore's *Life of Byron,* Beale's *Natural History of the Sperm Whale,* but Mangan?

While Herman Melville's literary reputation was being raised from near oblivion to preeminence during the 1920s James Clarence Mangan's critical rating was travelling the other way.

In 1992, with the exception of David Lloyd's illuminating *Nationalism and Minor Literature: James Clarence Mangan and the Emergence of Cultural Nationalism* (University of California Press, 1987), the man with the name so remarkably like *margin,* has been all but forgotten by serious literary criticism.

What is a parenthesis?

On a January morning, in the hushed privacy of the Anglo-European-American Houghton Library, I opened *Poems by James Clarence Mangan, with Biographical Introduction by John Mitchel* (New York: Haverty, 1859). I saw the pencilled trace of Herman Melville's passage through John Mitchel's introduction and knew by shock of poetry telepathy the real James Clarence Mangan is the progenitor of fictional Bartleby.

The problem was chronology.

Melville wrote "Bartleby, The Scrivener: A Story of Wall Street" during the summer of 1853.

* * *

Quite an Original

Melville's copy of *Poems by James Clarence Mangan* is second hand. A newspaper clipping about the poet is pasted to the inside cover under the first owner's name. J.G. Hefferman 1st Nov. '59. Hefferman's name has been lined out.

When Melville wrote his own name and Feb. 15, 1862, N.Y. on the front fly-leaf he was forty-three. On the title page under Mangan's name he has worked out the poet's dates in parenthesis in pencil.

(Died about	1848
Born	1803)
	45

I had spent the previous day looking over the many scrawled boxes, heavy lines, arrows, checks, and bursts of agreement or disagreement in the margins of Matthew Arnold's *Essays in Criticism*: this heavily scored paragraph from Mitchel's introduction, "James Clarence Mangan: His Life, Poetry, and Death," was a marked contradiction.

> The comparative unacquaintance, also, of Americans with these poems may be readily accounted for, when we remember how completely British criticism gives the law throughout the literary domain of that semi-barbarous tongue in which I have the honor to indite. For this Mangan was not only an Irishman, —not only an Irish papist, —not only an Irish papist rebel; —but throughout his whole literary life of twenty years, he never deigned to attorn to English criticism, never published a line in any English periodical, or through any Eng-

lish bookseller, never seemed to be aware that there was a British Public to please. He was a rebel politically, and a rebel intellectually and spiritually, —a rebel with his whole heart and soul against the British spirit of the age. The consequence was sure, and not unexpected. Hardly anybody in England knew the name of such a person; and the only critique of his volumes called "German Anthology" which I have ever met with, is a very short and contemptuous notice in the *Foreign Quarterly*, for October, 1845, wherein the austere critic declares Mr. Mangan's method of rendering the German to be, "not gilding refined gold, but plating it with copper; not painting the lily white, but plastering it with red ochre."

Mangan already had American readers during the 1850s, though it would be hard for us to know it now. This summer in Henry J. Donaghy's "Selected Bibliography" to *James Clarence Mangan* (Twayne Publishers, Inc., 1974) I found a reference to an article by Francis J. Thompson called "Mangan in America: 1850-1860," *Dublin Magazine* XXVII (1952). Thompson only briefly touches on Melville but he does demonstrate persuasively that Mangan's reputation was legendary among writers in New York City during the decade leading up to the Civil War. Thompson cites a series of articles called "Some Irish Poets" by Charles Carroll Leeds, published during 1851 in the *United States Magazine and Literary Review*. I managed to find the issues in the stacks of Sterling Library. Ten years before Melville acquired his poems, nearly two years before he wrote his "Story of Wall Street," in September, 1851, Edgar Allan Poe was being compared to James Clarence Mangan and Thomas Davis in the pages of the *United States Magazine and Literary Review*.[1] In the October, 1851, issue, "Some Irish Poets" was entirely devoted to Mangan. There Melville would have read of the Irish poet's occupation as scrivener, the "feminine softness of his voice," the political rebellion in his writing, and his death by starvation in the city of Dublin. Charles Carroll Leeds even supplied a bibliography.

By the time Melville acquired Mitchel's edition of Mangan's poems in 1862, he was already familiar with the poet's life and work.

* * *

[1]For a comprehensive assessment of Melville's love-hate relationship with *United States Magazine and Literary Review* see Michael Paul Rogin's *Subversive Genealogy: The Politics and Art of Herman Melville*, Berkeley: University of California Press, 1983, pp. 70-72, 150.

False fleeting perjured Clarence

Bartleby, China Aster, Frank, Beggar, Confidence Man, Imposter, Stephen Hero, Stephen Dedalus, Leopold Bloom, are you the father or the son?

I have traced what books I can find by or about you in America. I hope to return to Ireland someday but will always be a foreigner with the illusions of a tourist. In Dublin I may discover the undated third edition of *The Poets and Poetry of Ireland*, or something else. So far I have only seen one tattered shambles of a copy in the sub-section of Sterling Library where damaged books go for rebinding. Pages of "Fragments From An Unfinished Autobiography" are so brittle pieces break off when I turn.

Did you see the young Shelley in Dublin? Some say you influenced Poe, others say it goes the other way. You are everywhere in Joyce's writing.

Your sister is there in "Araby."

Recent books about you or your work are thin as physical Bartleby. Except for *Nationalism and Minor Literature: James Clarence Mangan and the Emergence of Irish Cultural Nationalism,* but that's in a wider series called "The New Historicism. Studies in Cultural Poetics."

"*Nationalism and Minor Literature* is a 'reorientation.'"

* * *

To find the empty vast and wand'ring air

"Giacomo Clarenzio Mangan"

> All his poetry records injustice and tribulation, and the aspiration of one who is moved to great deeds and rending cries when he sees in his mind the hour of his grief. This is the theme of a large part of Irish poetry, but no other poems are as full, as are those of Mangan, of misfortune nobly suffered, of vastation of soul so irreparable. Naomi wished to change her name to Mara, because she had known too well how bitter is the existence of mortals, and is it not perhaps a profound sense of sorrow and bitterness that explains in Mangan all the names and titles that he gives himself, and the fury of translation in which he tried to hide himself? For he did not find in himself the faith of the solitary, or the faith that in the Middle Ages sent the spires in the air like triumphant songs, and he waits his hour, the

hour that will end his sad days of penance. Weaker than Leopardi, for he has not the courage of his own despair, but forgets every ill and forgoes all scorn when someone shows him a little kindness, he has, perhaps for this reason, the memorial that he wished, a

[*one page missing*]

James Joyce, from "Giacomo Clarenzio Mangan," one of three public lectures in Italian at the Università Popolare in Trieste. 1904. Editorial note in brackets.

Before Modernism.

The eleventh edition of the *Encyclopaedia Britannica* (1911) says his fame has been deferred by the inequality and mass of work, much of it lying buried in inaccessible newspaper files under so many pseudonyms . . . .

"Lamii's Apology for his Nonsense, (From the Ottoman.)"

The pale bright margins

*　　　*　　　*

"Se Dedalo ingegnoso, ai Fianchi uni."

In Sonnet XVIII., seeing an eagle soaring over his head, he thinks how happy it is for the birds that they can pass from one country to another without being arrested on their way by a demand for "Three Giulii."

In the next novel thought strikes him, and —

"The Three Half-Crowns."

*　　　*　　　*

The book of life and out

of the

The book of life and out

Four blank pages are bound in here

in my arms

of the holy city and from

All my soul is in the book

the things that are written

in this book

2.

I think him to be natural
deeply by those books
In those places think him to be
In those breaks and pauses
Turned to the boats
that landscape meets air
I could only plan
All other simulacra
marked then ERASED
Some green forest annotation
failed have forgotten
Between two negations
horror of the world
Could not leave the world

The salary coyly said yes
Drag handcuff along fence
or you in it all tractable
Awry pulled up by cinchstrap
yes buckled to the capital
green worth say yes English
a certain mock hobo bravado
mean scrip so solitary wroth
Darkening noon changed he s
untractable in darkness un
manacled beside the capital
he s waging political babble
a context goes awry in novel
He took out American money

Question of a happy life
any asylum in moderation
Object is something erased
is character the opposite
An author-evacuated text
triple-checked double-marked
Ghost of one's own glory
into the subjectless abject
by distance or by stillness
sleep gone steering row
Title of an After-Thought
he put a veil on his face - minister's
black veil
Hawthorne

Wearied human language
take me so that I no longer
am perpetually dispersed
and appear not to know
When I wander far off
roughened and wrought human
to the matter of fact
Refuting and chastising
Love a secret between two
Certainty decreed to go
They are always masked

Wakefield "I shall soon go back"
The leaf s turned down
Loatheness to do
Tracking a favorite writer
in the snow (as Dryden expresses it
of others
I subscribe
For you
Una is dressed in exile
and theoretical austerity
She is haunting
the Pantheon

Morality I will not thought

Along the glistening shore

we tramp to leave their print

Melville the source hunter

hawking corollaries for coal

foraging for fuel in copses

What a semi-barbarous ballad

Saw that the saw sawed thought

Skipping oblivion for forfeit

Wide universe no matter what

that their thought may go out

the margin s mile of welcome

A full stop at *Pursue*
for some occult reason
And two false starts
of line 2 with *Angel*

The beautiful passage in *Prometheus*
The nether millstone

Narcis if I h

"Forct" in copy

"h" from bough

Thissby this

hishis spirit

I th For th

If I am the N

This is an error

Fy

Shelley's pen slipped
referring to the Sun
Isle Continent Ocean
The date July 1st 1822
across "?fury" may be
"day" or "fiery"
by mischief superimposed on *wild*
tercet mask tercet

Travelling in the direction
of an imagination of morning
he was brought back mortal
Struck against parenthesis
across an anarchy of light
Dare I uncreate Prometheus
Chorus Semichorus Semichorus
flame in greek by a copyist

Shelleyan but may be Mary
Traces u pon the comin g
east above the clouds now
a doodle meadow in pencil
the bracket isn t closed
Mary tried to mend “wrecht”

ame n of hal f l ight
alter wi t hwillow
? water stain to right
may again echo mary
spotted palmate orchis
Au dictors can not
if Poetry

Coffin th sea

Coffin th se a

Coffin th s   wooD

ir e wr t ebly quell

in pencil s c atte

but poetry

Coffin th se aw

Coffin th se w

Coffin th se woorD

Walking the whole time
beside fears of danger
we come to a headland
source of all that past
Look boldly at futurity
at the iron issue of necessity
originality dies out
an essay on Epitaphs
Subversion was an emblem
The owl beats its way
hangs affrighted to sky
The obscurity is poetry
Oh Shelley remote alloy
refine love love loyalty

One forever occupied
stood on the path
with whispered information
that that person
was Clarence Mangan
a spectral creature on a ladder
all his soul was in the book
in his arms
Roisin Dubh means Ireland
On earth I guess
I am bound by a definition
of criticism

Roosting on a ladder
for several months
even several years
the librarian Mangan
roved through languages
an unearthly figure
in a brown garment
The same garment
to all appearances
which lasted until
the day of his death
The blanched hair
was totally unkempt
The corpse-like features
as still as marble

Instead of classifying
he browsed and dreamed
he didn't even browse
regularly

Mangan was not the polyglot
he pretended to be
Translations were the rage
of the moment
and he turned them out
as regularly and as competently
as he had turned out
acrostics some years before
From 1837 onwards
Mangan deluged
the *Dublin University Magazine*
with "translations"
from the Turkish Arabic Persian
Welsh Coptic Danish French German
Russian Spanish Swedish Frisian
Bohemian

Ask not nor task not
A polyglot anthology
out of no materials
is absolute derision
What nondescript yell
in treasonable Bohemian
and if the Modeem of
Alystan be kith or
kin of mine let dust
derange so ever darker
the glory of my hair
Simile is always poetry

I hate scenery and sun
half-whimsically if be
If I be clear what is Moore
derision half-seriously
House if the reader please
hovel to his originals'
What is a parenthesis.
Long passage on fallacy
hypochondriasis despair
the "Sarasenic world" &
Ind & other Ottoman airs
On the field at Mallach-brack
my shibboleth is refrain
Put my black wig back on

The period 1840-42
was for Mangan one of drift
of aimlessness of deterioration
he lodged badly
he ate badly
his letters are usually short notes
asking for money
or acknowledging it
they make doleful reading
Mangan revelled in the expression
of passionate sorrow
he loved to loose himself
In Ireland's past and future
To go astray in the world
to forget it

Sect him I cannot
to go skin deep two
in his triune cloak
for selfsame Selber
a German derivative
the poet-Cain's crime
Dash to the right Kathaleen
Ny—is the feminine
Mr. Editor you took
the part where four
roads meet Scattery
Drumcliffe Ratoo—My
grief to you Kilroy
Penny submission Aladdin

He rode his hobby a
round Fagel Library
unallied unhousel'd
under the Poor Law
My mind has no home
the dead face orient
I will "do" the song
out of the Jacobite
Counterfeit when you
look artist of Sais
My mind is its Cain
a semiocomic Paradox
Pun someone someone
Cimmerian garden Aladdin

"A sea of argument stretches out
before us
and the waves thereof curl
about our feet
But we forbear to plunge in
Reflection recurs
and we receive a *check*
on the *bank*"

Typological disdain of human applause
is the only great thing
about him
except his cloak
he said of his home-made poet
"Selber"

"Before encasing our pen we
cannot avoid averting with
regret to the apathy of our
contemporaries English and
Irish on the subject of
foreign literature Is it not
shameful we should have been
left to fight our Oriental
battles alone? According to
Vallency every Irishman is
an Arab yet what Irishman has
come forward to second our
exertions"

"Nine-twentieths of those
allusions to wine and wine
bibbing which startle us in
writings of Mohammedan poets
are regarded by Sir William
Jones and other competent
authorities as susceptible of
a figurative interpretation
To acknowledge the truth at the
close of our paper we dislike
Eastern poetry Mysticism and
stupidity are synonymous terms
in our vocabulary"

There were then as I
have said two Mangans
one well known to the
Muses the other to the
Police the one soared
through the empyrean
and sought the stars
the other too often
lay in the gutters of
Peter Street and Bride Street
He had a haven in
the Ordnance Survey
Office where he was at
peace among topographers
and antiquaries

I read at another time
that he resided in a
hay-loft nothing very
definite ever happened to
him absent-minded and no
stranger to hospitals
Mangan perished suddenly
and quietly on the 20th
of July 1849 his life
went out at the Meath
Hospital Long Lane he was
buried in Glasnevin Cemetery
Three persons are said to
have followed his remains
to the grave

The longevity of the Irish
how Saints Mochta Ciaran
Brendan in a time of fast
reply a little bit of meat
Shrine doorway tower ruin
Drudge dole pauper famine
I too have been a dreamer
and am seeking a spiritual
leader on the ground and in
air out in perpetual weather
Regions of Araby the blest
royal descent for all of us

Evening outruns Cain
as far as the author
with his banishment
went out whithersoever
Pelican of the universe
one of broken purpose
love its own allegory
end of the Apocrypha
He also did predestinate
the righteous Abel
Call evil good good evil
We admirers of Faust
so inexpressibly wary
have no room for emptiness
in the sense of rest

—Byron's venetian episode
how on the wild island
enclosed like Phaeton
in all-consuming flesh
that melancholy exile
stood where Byron stood
The melancholia of Byron
A passage between them
in common in marginalia
We track our own desire
pursuit and Diana paradox
as in old emblem books
"vanitas vanitatum vanitas"
Who could know better
good evil evil good dualism

In the domestic interest
he confines Beatrice
Veil and concealment
torn before she turns
She consults her brother
They hire murderers
Theology legal philosophy
Tabernacle of the sun
Nations by light of it
each reader or marauder
reading over then over
Archives of the Cenci
the father Count Cenci
Unfilial someone self
my next attempt will be a *Life*

Etiology says that increasingly
in the marvelous group *Laocöon*
those two marble snakes surely will
strangle him and his children
Wrapped in the "Nacheträglichkeit"
they are the "manacles of love"
So often I will write all day
So rearrange all piteous recoil
So essay caustic perjured mirth
perilous mirth of Jacobean tragedy
Revellers and masqueraders you
equivocating witches in *Macbeth*
no cloak smothers my mirth I am
the sublimated mother of Jocasta
No verse over against this heath

Tradition wild imagination
at least I can speak out
though I preach to myself
too many brief chronicles
about the thread of life
Quick-witted at threading
Reason watches no doubt
other doubt ad infinitum
Personality or what man is
I went and viewed the wall
Enunciated anagram confine
in clenched fist pamphlets
philosophy is comfortless
the idol political justice

Quarry of his experience
The delirium of enthusiasm
is the victim of feeling
so love so frail confine
Something orthodox an order
sequence canto sonnet cut
under this reading an author
infinite fate straw habit
Found for what was hiding
Wrack human sea keep back
this ghost of my illusion
Unvisited remote wide anarchy
Childe Harold is a pilgrim
Dominion sere imagination

Because he stole the light
my heart is feminine
What meaning is there
in my head my clothing
Unconfined as an ocean
nerves are what they are
delusions of imagination
Hero of authentic poetry
I can compose my thought
an excursus on Tradition
trace of the word *city*
I will dismember marginalia
'l' for 'i' and 'i' for 'l'
Ophelia Juliet Cordelia

Printing ruins it
It is as its edge
Faun ink splatter
all that antiquity
no name I remember
It could be Panthea
It could be Imogen
on the inked hyphen
Spatter constellate
we are so barefoot
The rest is in rime
or footprint or Pan
in ink on scrap it
never unbidden Imogen

Brute alternate heart
whose child I won
whose aspect wore
in doubling combat
with Night <u>un</u>carnate
Skittish the owl
the nightingale only
Soothe say a wild
an unimagined song
Now which nine ages
I am far too copy
Certain it is wild
Who will be signal
Narcissus you are free

Come afterward compiler
the impediment of words
torn to pieces by memory
No questions unanswered
there is no contending
Sheer off and avoid him
voiceless reclusion veil
Between ourself and the story
so low almost a whisper
Lyric for crossing over
where he dreamed he was
I put down my thoughts
Vulturism trimmed for binding
who will be interpreter

Spoke of the hearts of the poor
Light in which we were rushing
Life is so the merchant either
gains the shore both hands full
of dollars or else one day waves
wash him up on that sandbar so
what and Massinger smiled and he
said you know print settles it
Out of view of the rushing light
print is sentinel so sages say
Dollars he said and hoped they'd
have made a bed for him then he
would call whatever gaol a goal
Obedience we are subjects Susan
Scared millions and on he rushed